Famous Jatras of Nepal

Some Jatras in Nepal Which You Must Know About

Asmita Jha

pencil

ISBN 978-93-5667-660-2
© Asmita Jha 2023

Published in India 2023 by Pencil

Contributors:
Editor: Susmita Jha

A brand of
One Point Six Technologies Pvt. Ltd.
Unit no. 26, Ground Floor, Building A1,
Wadala Truck Terminal Road,
Near Post Office, Antop Hill, Mumbai - 400037
E connect@thepencilapp.com
W www.thepencilapp.com

DISCLAIMER: *The opinions expressed in this book are those of the authors and do not purport to reflect the views of the Publisher.*

Author biography

I, Asmita Jha is an inhabitant of Nepal. From childhood, I am living in Kathmandu valley. I am interested in exploring the Nepali cultures. Moreover, I think that these traditions should be continued as they help us in remembering our historical times. Also, I believe that this can help in introuducing Nepal to the whole world.

CONTENTS

Ropain Jatra or Mud Festival or Rice Planting Festival

When?

Asadh 15

Why this date?

Asadh, the 3rd month according to the Nepalese calendar is the best month for planting rice. This is because the rain helps flood the lands, creating an ideal environment sot that rice saplings would germinate.

Why?

1-Previously, agriculture was the major occupation of Nepal.

-Many farmers depended on agriculture to earn their livelihood.

-They kept the cultivated crops for their families as well as for distribution if needed.

2-Men used to keep the rice fields arable to plant them by ploughing the fields and arranging for the drainage systems.

-Women used to take care of the actual planting of the saplings of rice.

Where?

Khokana, Kirtipur, Lalitpur, and Bhaktapur.

How?

-At least 1 member of the family should take part in rice planting on this day.
-They eat Dahi Chiura (Chiura: beaten rice, Dahi: curd) along with the fruits, particularly bananas.
-Even songs and dances are performed.
-They play with mud as well.
-Some people also try Chhyang (alcohol brewed locally).
Who celebrates?
Nepali farmers
Belief:
The tradition of rice planting can be preserved.

References:
https://holidays.buddhaair.com/blog/ropain-jatra-in-nepal-a-mud-festival

Dahi Jatra (or Curd-Splashing Festival

-Curd is also known as Yoghurt or Dahi which is made from milk and is sour.

-This festival is similar to the 'La Tomatina' festival in Spain where the participants throw tomatoes among themselves just for fun.

When?
One day after Bijaya Dashami.

Where?
Tauthali village in Nepal

Which god/goddess is worshipped?
Tripura Sundari Mai

Who Celebrates?
Inhabitants of Tauthali

How?
-The participants throw curd among themselves for fun as well as for fulfilling the tradition.

-On the day of Ekadashi, the body of participants along with the whole temple of Shree Tripura Sundari Maai is filled with curd.

How was it originated?

-In the 13th century during Malla Rule, the farmers kept cattle to offer curd to the goddess so that they would be blessed to produce more curd the next year.

A Variation from Ancient Time

-In ancient times, it was seen that after this jatra, a stream of curd flowed down in this area. However, because of the reduction in the number of farmers rearing cattle, the amount of curd has decreased.

-Curd is also known as Yoghurt or Dahi which is made from milk and is sour.

-This festival is similar to the 'La Tomatina' festival in Spain where the participants throw tomatoes among themselves just for fun.

References:

https://en.wikipedia.org/wiki/Dahi_Jatra

Kha Me Jatra

What is meant by 'Kha Me'?
-The word Kha Me' refers to the pure male buffalo without any physical defects or wounds.
-This buffalo is considered the symbol of Mahisasura, the demon.
-The buffalo should have 7 chakras.
-Its hair in the middle and front parts should lean to the front.
-On the other hand, the hair at the back should lean to the back.

When?
Nawami, the ninth day of Dashain

Where?
Bhaktapur (Jatra) and Panauti (Puja)

Who celebrates?
-The Banamala clan, a sub-group in the Newar community. They rear the buffalo in the name of the goddess 'Brmhyayani', especially for the festival. They tie the buffalo with the rope in the pillar of the temple if the type of buffalo described above is not found.

How?

-The buffalo is taken to Dattatreya Square (Gathemung) near the Durga temple.

-On the evening of Nawami, it is taken to the open street.

-The buffalo is fed with alcohol to make it drunk.

-Then, it is chased by the people from the temple of goddess Durga to Bramhayani temple.

-When it is chased, it is taken to Hanumante River (1 kilometre away from Durga temple) for cleaning. The pilgrims take bath here as well.

-Magical rituals are conducted by sprinkling the holy water in that river along with the flowers and rice on the buffalo's body whispering some tantric mantra in its ear.

-Its head is worshipped as a Mahisasura demon and its body is distributed to the people in the form of prasad. It is said that this holy Prasad helps in eliminating the evils in the family.

-This Prasad is also stored and burnt in the form of incense in the fire of Lakshmi Puja in Tihar.

Belief:

-The Prasad (meat from the body of Kha Me) helps in keeping away the evils from the family.

References:

https://en.wikipedia.org/wiki/Khame_Jatra

https://www.nepjol.info/index.php/litstud/article/view/39529

Gahana Khojne Jatra (The Jatra of Searching Jewels)

Where?
Gahanapokhari pond, Hadigaun, Kathmandu

Who is worshipped?
Goddess, Tundaldevi/Baishnodevi

When?
Chaitra Shukla Astami (The 8th day before Full moon in Chaitra)

From when?
The Time of the Kirat Dynasty

Who celebrate it?
Newar Community

What is done?
- The youths carry the palaki/rath of Tundaldevi on their shoulders and take around the pond 'Gahanapokhari' 3 times.
-Moreover, they play the Newari musical instruments like Nyakhin and Dhime.

-They provide offerings and pay homage to the goddess.

Belief:

While carrying the palaki of 'Tundaldevi' on their shoulders, they search for the lost jewels in Gahanapokhari.

References:

https://ekantipur.com/photo_feature/2023/04/07/16808 8084924379658.html

https://imagepasal.com/photo/gahana-khojne-jatra-gahana-pokhari-kathmandu/#:~:text=Gahana%20Khojne%20Jatra%20(se arching%20for,community%20of%20Hadigaun%2C%20K athmandu%20city.

Temal Jatra

When?
Chaitra Shukla Purnima

Where?
-Shwayambhu and Bouddha in Kathmandu
-Nowadays, it is also celebrated at Sindhupalchok, Kavrepalanchok, Rasuwa, Nuwakot, Makwanpur, Dhading, Lalitpur, etc.

Who does this?
Tamang community of Nepal

What is done?
1. Chaturdashi (1 day before the full moon)
-During the evening of Chaturdashi, people light diyo ('deep prajwalan') at Bouddha Chaitya.
2. Purnima (Full moon)
-Those who had lit diyo the previous day take bath at Baishdhara in the morning on this day.
-Some people even perform visit the Jamacho of Nagarjun and perform worship at Shwayambhu Chaitya after that on the same day.
-Those who can't go to Nagarjun conduct worship at the Shwayambhu Chaitya after taking bath.

-To go to Jamacho, nowadays, the checkpost of the Nepal army is opened at Raniban on the day of Chaitra Shukla Purnima only.

How was it originated?
-During Satyayug, 'Bipaswi Buddha' planted a lotus in the pond ('daha') of the valley. From that day, this jatra is celebrated.
-It was named 'Temal Jatra' at the time of King Rinjin Dorje, the last king of Temal. In 1819 B.S., he gave royal importance to this jatra and sent the citizens to celebrate this jatra in the Bouddha area.

References:

https://ekantipur.com/photo_feature/2023/04/07/16808
8084924379658.html
https://imagepasal.com/photo/gahana-khojne-jatra-
gahana-pokhari-
kathmandu/#:~:text=Gahana%20Khojne%20Jatra%20(se
arching%20for,community%20of%20Hadigaun%2C%20K
athmandu%20city.

Bisket Jatra Biska Jatra

-Also known as 'Satruhanta Jatra' due to the belief that on observing this jatra, the enemies go away.

When?
--Starts 4 days before the new year
--Continues for 9 days and 8 nights.

What is done?
-People move around various areas in Bhaktapur during this jatra.
-People play with Sindur (a holy powder, crimson-coloured, mainly put in the siudo by married women).
-Some people pierce their tongues ('jibro chhedne').
-In Madhyapur Thimi, other jatra like Sindur jatra, Bishnuvir Jatra, Chanhesiya jatra (at night), and Siddhikali jatra are celebrated as well during this Bisket jatra.

First Day
-In the evening, the rath of Nakinju Ajima is taken from the 5-storeyed temple of Tamari to 'Ghatkha'. Then, the rath of Bhairavnath is pulled and the jatra is started.
-The main god and 'Betal god' of Bhairavnath are put in the rath and then it is taken from the topmost floor of the temple ('Thane') and lowermost ('Quane') to the tole by pulling.

-Before pulling the cart, the god 'Bhairavnath' is worshipped and the weapons 'Khadga, sword, and nishan' are kept on the rath.

-The rath is taken to either the lower tole or upper tole. The tole in which it is taken is considered the winning tole.

5th Day of Bisket Jatra, The Nepali New Year: Baisakh 1

-One day before it, 55-hands tall Lingo is put up ('uthayinxa'). (lingo uthaune karyakram) by following various rituals near the Mahalaxmi temple of Bode.

-After that, the people pierce their tongues. Thus, the jatra of piercing tongue ('jibro chhedne jatra') is also believed to have started after putting up this lingo.

-The real jatra starts in the Thimi area after this Lingo is put up by the locals.

-Fairs are organized in the temples.

-Moreover, feasts (bhoj) are conducted.

-On this day, Lingo is blown down ('dhalinxa').

-Before putting down the Lingo, the worship of Bahrav and Betal is performed.

-After putting it down, the rath of Bhairabnath and Bhadrakali is taken to Gahity and coincided with each other.

-On this night, the worship is done for the goddess 'Dumaju' in the Taleju temple by following the rituals and jatra is performed after that.

Last Day of Jatra

-The rath of Bhairavnath is taken from the Thane and Quane toles like the first day by pulling to take it again to the Bhairavnath temple of Tamari.

Security Provided during the Jatra:
-More than 1000 armies are hired because:

--At night time, many people die when pressed by the rath.

--Also, the houses may be turned down during the jatra resulting in much destruction.

Beliefs:
-Enemies go away when the jatra is conducted.

-It is believed that during the pulling of rath, the mouths of Bhimsen temple (present in front of Dattatraya temple) and Betal should not coincide.

Rath:
-It is 3-storeyed.

-It is made of wood.

-It is constructed in Pagoda style.

-It has 5 long ropes at the front and 4 at the back.

-The peple involved in the jatra pull the rath with the help of those ropes and take it to their toles.

-The main thing in the jatra is the pulling of the rath.

 -Some youths begin to throw stones at each other during the jatra.

Bisket Jatra in Britain in 2079
-The program was organized by 'Pasa Puchah Guthi', UK.

-In the 'Asian community hall' of South-East London, the Newar community were dressed in cultural dresses.

-They also pulled Rath in this jatra around the hall for 12 minutes.

-They took 20 days to make the khat.

-Moreover, Newari dishes were cooked during the jatra.

-650 people were involved.

-This has made the jatra famous even abroad in the belief of protecting the culture.

History

-Based on Bikram Sambat, this jatra is celebrated based on 'Sauryamas' as the belief of 'Bihsit' (meaning the snake died) from the Lichhavi period.

-In Thimi based on the Tamsuk Patra (a historical paper of Nepal Sambat 500), this jatra is believed to use 'Bishik' words for making the 'Bishwa Ketu' understand the meanings.

-It is also called 'Bishwojatra' based on the 'Silalekh' (written on the stone) at Taumadi of Bhaktapur created during the period of Yaksha Malla.

-In the writ (abhiseka) at the period of Kings Jitamitra and Bhupatindra Malla during Nepal Sambat 808 and 818 respectively, 'Bishkyat' words are written.

References:

https://www.onlinekhabar.com/2022/04/1108534
https://www.onlinekhabar.com/2022/04/1107635
https://www.onlinekhabar.com/2022/04/1107189
https://www.onlinekhabar.com/2021/04/945238

Gaijatra

-Called as 'Saparu' in Newari community.

When?

8 days from Bhadra Krishna Pratipada (the first day after the full moon in the month 'Bhadra' in the Nepali calendar') onwards. It falls on the second day of Janaipurnima/Rakshabandhan.

--There is a public holiday in Nepal on the second day of Rakshabandhan/the first day of Gaijatra.

Where?

--Mainly in Bhaktapur.

--Also celebrated in Parsa, Dang, Palpa, Morang, Kaski, Ilam, Khotang, Nuwakot, Bhaktapur, Sindhupalchok, Sunsari, Makwanpur, Kavre, along with Katmandu and Lalitpur.

What is done?

-During gaijatra, the Newar community people decorate the person in the form of a cow and take them around their area in memory of their dead beloved ones.

-They offer milk, fruits, beaten rice (chiura), curd, fruits, and materialistic offerings.

-In Bhaktapur, people also perform 'Jhaki' around the city along with musical instruments.

-Also, some people take the live cow or cow made of clay or unmarried girls (kumari kanya) around the city during this duration.

Dances Performed during Gaijatra:
-Ghintangkisi (for seven days)
-Mak Pyakh

Belief:
1-When the person in the form of a cow is taken around the area, then the person who has died in that year can go to heaven by touching the cow's tail. (Baitarani paar garxan)
2-Based on the old Hindu literature, it is said that the main gate of Yamlok (the palace of Lord Yama, the god of death) is closed for the whole year. However, when the Gaijatra is done on the earth (Prithivilok/Matrayalok), this gate is opened and the dead souls get a chance to enter Yamalok and get 'mukti' (freedom).

Story:
-When the son of King Pratap Malla died, his queen was in deep shock. So, the king tried to show her that other many people also have to face the same incident. For this, he ordered the countrypeople 'perform gaijatra in the memory of your beloved dead ones'. In this way, Gaijatra was started.
-Even after this, the queen could not recover. Hence, the king made the tradition of laughing and satire programs ('hasyabyangatmak karyakram') on this day. Thus, dances are shown. Moroever, satirical comments are given against social evils. Moreover, the songs of Ramayana are sung.

-From that time, Gaijatra is conducted through the 'Rajprasad' at Hanumandhoka till now.

How was it originated?

-It is said that King Pratap Malla and the Gopal dynasty ordered to not tell that the Gaijatra began during their period.

-In the 'Patra 61' (a paper written 600 years ago) of the Gopal dynasty during the ruling period of Jayasthiti Malla, the term 'Saan Yat' is mentioned. This means 'Gai Jatra'. Thus, Gai Jatra is considered to have begun before the period of Jayasthiti Malla.

-Some people believe it began before the 14th century at the end of the Licchavi dynasty.

Contributors for Gai Jatra:

-King Pratap Malla of Kathmandu

-King Jagatprakash Malla of Bhaktapur

-King Siddhinarsingh Malla of Lalitpur.

Gaijatra by Rare Sexes

-The intersexual people, 3rd sex people and homosexual people call this day as 'pride day'.

-The organization 'Nil Hira Samaj' in Nepal organizes rallies for the rights of such people from 'Sanchaykosh Bhawan' of Thamel to 'Tundikhel' through Basantapur.

-After the rally, they also perform musical events.

-In ancient times, Nepali society didn't even touch the dead body of rare sex people. Hence, for the peace of the dead soul, this day is celebrated.

An Interesting Event During Corona in Gaijatra:
-Mask and face shields were worn by people instead of mukundo (crown).

References:
https://www.onlinekhabar.com/2020/08/886926
https://www.onlinekhabar.com/2020/08/887036
https://www.onlinekhabar.com/2022/08/1172544
https://www.onlinekhabar.com/2022/08/1172513

Ghodejatra

-Celebrated on 'Chaitra Krishna Aunshi' every year.

Story:

-Once upon a time, a devil named 'Gurumapa' used to live under a tree in the east-west direction in Tundikhel. He used to eat small children in the town. Thus, the local victims destroyed him. However, they had fear that the ghost of that devil might affect their children again. Hence, every year, on the day of Krishna Aunsi of Chaitra, the people conduct 'ghodejatra' with a belief that the 'taap' of the horse can dominate the soul of that devil. (ghoda ko taap le kulchayera dabaune gurmapa ko atma lai). Due to this, the children can be safe for the whole year.

-Moreover, for keeping the children safe, at the root of the tree, a little rice and meat of he-buffalo are offered to the 'Gurumapa' devil.

What is done?

-On this day, various events are shown at Tundikhel like:

a. Ashwakala

b. Motorcycle game

c. Physical exercise

d. Yuddhakala

e. Cross-Tent Pegging

f. Musical Ride

g. Cross-Country Jump

h. Group Jump

i. Hungarian post

-The president, vice-president, chief minister and other government officials come to watch ghodejatra on this day.

-Also, the skills of the dog are shown as the dog is a faithful and honest animal.

-On this day, a public holiday is given to the inhabitants of Kathmandu Valley.

Ghodejatra in Lalitpur

-In Lalitpur too, a 'kano' horse is run. Kano horse is a horse that appears as drunk.

-The ghodejatra is shown from Mangalbazar to Balkumari.

-The jatra is started from the main chowk of Mangalnbazar and ends at Balkumari taking the routes of Neut, Lohalan, Olkhu, and Bhol Ganesh.

-The horse is taken around the 'Siwacha' temple of Balgkumari 3 times and then returned to Bholhok. At Bholdhoka too, 3 rounds are taken.

-After that, Sagun is given to the Guthiyar, the one who sits on the horse.

-In Lalitpur, the ghodejatra is shown on only one horse.

-This is run by the Bhimsen Guthi of Jyapu tole at Balkumari.

-This jatra is conducted from the Malla period.

-The people (patra) of Mahabharat are considered in this jatra.

-Ghodejatra of Lalitput is considered to be older than that in Tundikhel of Kathmandu.

-It is believed to be started by the Chya Khalah (Newari phrase for the khalak of servants).

-The horse is taken from the cavalry of the Nepal army.

-One day before the jatra, the Jyapu community sacrifice the he-buffalo at Bhisensthan. The process is called 'Chhwayalabhu'.

-At Bhimsensthan, the idols of the 5 Pandavas are kept.

-The sacrificed he-buffalo is burnt north of 'Krishna Degal'.

-The belief is that Krishna killed the 'Kichak' devil in Mahabharat.

-Moreover, the bhajans are done one day before the jatra about this story.

-Then, the worship of 5 Pandavas is done at the Guthi and 'samaybaji' is given as the Prasad.

-The person who sits on the horse is respectfully given garland and put 'Tika'.

References:

https://ekantipur.com/photo_feature/2023/03/21/16793 9766901287.html

https://www.onlinekhabar.com/2022/04/1103149

https://www.onlinekhabar.com/2022/04/1103154

https://www.onlinekhabar.com/2021/04/944795

Seto Machhindranath Jatra

-Generally, in this jatra, the girls are involved in controlling the crowd during the jatra, as when the boys try to stop making the place crowdy, people take it in the form of ego.

When?
-The pulling of rath starts from Chaitra Shukla Astami.

Description of Rath/Chariot
-Nine-levelled (storeyed)
-36 hands tall, each level should be 4 hands tall traditionally.
-All levels have their meaning
-The storeys are designed based on tantrabidhi (some mythical rituals).
-'Chukul' (bolt) is required to stop the rath. It is a piece of wood with a bid made of iron which is carried by the youths sitting at the right and left of the rath so that they can stop the rath immediately whenever required. This acts as the brake of the rath.
-The wheels help in maintaining the speed of the rath.
-Gamah byabasthapan (management) is required for detecting in which direction the rath should be taken. Ghamah is the front part of the rath. The management should be done carefully as even if there is any issue in applying the technique the rath may fall. Thus, a stronger

team is required for that. The people involved in the ghamah byabasthapna perform the work of putting and taking out the rope, operating the chukul, and putting the brake on the rath.

Description of Jatra

-It continues for 4 days.

-However, sometimes the length may be increased if the rath is damaged. The length of the jatra may make it expensive.

-The jatra should be continued until the rath reaches its appropriate place.

Description of God

-Mahabihar at the middle of Asan and Indrachowk.

-It takes an area of 2 ropanis.

-It was made during the Lichhavi period.

-Inside the Mahabihar, a white idol, 5 feet tall is present.

-The god is decorated with various ornaments and dresses.

-The idol faces downwards. This indicates that the god looks towards the earth.

-The god is considered as 'Vishnu' by Vaishnavas, Shiva by Shaivas, Energy (Shakti) by Shaaktas, Sun (surya) by Saur, Brahma by Brahmins, Lokeshwor by Baidiks, and Karunamaya by Boudhas.

What is done?

-First day

-- The rath is taken from Jamal to Ason taking the route of Ratnapark and Bhotahity.

--When it is taken to Ason, the President views it.

--Previously, the king used to observe it at Ason.

-Second Day
--It is taken to Kaalbhairav taking the route of Makhan, Keltole, Balkumari, and Indrachowk and kept there.

-Third-Day
--From Kalbhairav, it is taken to Lagan through the route of Maruganesh, Jaishideval, and Janabahal.
--It is believed that the mother of Matsyendranath is present at Lagan.
-It is taken around Lagan 3 times.

-Fourth Day
--The Matsyendranath is worshipped on this day and taken out by putting it in small 'Khat'.
-Then it is taken to the Mahabihar of Kanak Chaitya present at Janabahal.
-It is not taken inside Bihar. However, it is kept near Bihar.

-Fifth Day
--Some worships like 'Hom', 'Shanti Puja', etc. are done and the god is kept at its original place.
--To keep the idol in the rath, the priest takes carries it by putting in small khat and takes it to Jamal.

Who does what?
a. Artists
-The artist makes the 'eye' of the god on the wheel of the rath.
-The eye is considered the symbol of 'naga' (snake).

b. Kansakar

-The kansakar blows musical instruments during the rath yatra.

c. Shakya

-They do worship-related work.

d. Munikar

-They manage the flowers.

e. Jyapu

-The most responsible community during this jatra.

-At each storey of the rath, only Jyapu farmers can sit.

f. Manandhar

-Do the work of dakarmi (Mason).

-Also, they collect the wood for the rath.

-Moreover, they check whether the wood is suitable or not.

-If the wood is not suitable, another wood is brought.

-They are also involved in putting the 'inla' made of silver over the god.

-Also, they put the 'tundal' at the main gate.

How was it originated?

-When a Jyapu farmer was digging his field at Jamal, the idol of Seto Machhindranath was found. The people were worried about where to keep the idol. In the meeting, the priest at that time, 'Nilkaji Shakya' told them that the king was told in his dreams to put the idol at Chaitya Mahabihar. Thus, it was kept at Mahabihar. As it was found at Jamal, the rath yatra starts from here.

Trouble during the Ancient times:

-When the rath touched the houses, there occurred disputes.

References:

https://ekantipur.com/national/2023/04/02/1680405771
46791637.html

https://ekantipur.com/national/2023/04/02/1680405771
46791637.html

Khat Jatra

Where?

Ward Number 5 of Lalitpur.

-This is called the 'khat yatra' of devi 'Mahalaxmi'.

Who celebrate it?

-Celebrated by 'Kayaguni Manka: Khala:'

-Mahalaxmi temple is located in between the northern part of the ring road and Lagankhel.

When?

Ramnavami

What is done?

-On the day of Ramnavami, Goddess Mahalaxmi is worshipped by the method of rituals and this Jatra is started from the temple of Thasikhel.

-The goddess is decorated artistically and taken around many 'tole' (places) of the Patan city.

-After taking around the toles, the idol is taken to the 'Mahashaktipith' of Patan.

-The various Mahashaktipith are 'Chamunda Mai' in Shankhamul (north), 'Balkumari Mai' in Balkumari (east), and Bishnudevi Mai in Nakkhu (West).

-In the Khat, 12 different goddesses are put.

-One week before the jatra, the idols of the goddess are coloured in the house of the priest (pujari/Dhyala:).

-Each year, the artists from the 'Hogal tole' are called for the colouring purpose.

-The goddess is taken to the houses of artists. This arrangement is done by 'Manka Khal'.

-From their house, the idol is put in 'Kharpan' and again taken to Kayagunni Khal and put in the house of 'Kaji Chhe'.

-On the day of Chaite Dashain (Astami), the idol is kept in the house of Kaji Chhe'.

-In the morning of Navami, Bhajan is started.

-After that, the idol is taken in Khat from the house of Kaji Chhe to the Mahalaxmi temple.

-After that, she is worshipped by following the necessary rituals.

-In the afternoon, 'baji' is distributed as the 'prasad' of Mahalaxmi.

-After serving baji, the goddess is taken froom the temple to 'jajman'.

-The jajaman puts the idol in the KHat.

-After that, the pujari faints (loses consciousness).

-Then, the pujari is woken up by sprinkling water brought from the pipalbot near the temple.

-After putting the idol In the khat, the idol is taken around the temple 3 times.

-In the evening, the pulling of the khat is started.

-The 'toli' group is taken forward by blowing the musical instruments like 'dhime baja', basuri, and 'Nayakhi'.

-After that, the path of Namsangit is conducted followed by the artists.

-The other day, the khat is taken to the pujari's house. This work is done by 'Thati Dhyala puch'.

-The puch in the Thati tole takes the idol around the various toles of Ptan and then again taken to the priest's house. This is generally accomplished by the Jyapu community.

-This jatra is generally conducted at night time.

Difference from the Past Days

-In the past, it used to be celebrated at 9 p.m. It used to become midnight for taking around the idol around the tole and Shakti pith. However, nowadays, this jatra is conducted in the daytime only and ended in the evening.

-In the past, the people used to beg in various houses for worship ('puja magne chalan'). Nowadays, it is not done.

-It is now becoming rare because of financial reasons. It generally takes around 8 lakhs for this work.

-The goddess is called Mahalxami by Hindus and 'Basundhara' by 'Buddhamargi'.

References:

https://ekantipur.com/national/2023/03/30/1680142072
93941667.html

https://www.nepalnews.com/s/capital/chamunda-
rathyatra-celebrated-in-boudhha-jorpati-area

Khadga Jatra or Paya

-Different methods in Hindu and Boudha religions.
-This jatra shows the difference between 'madhu' and 'sura'.

What is meant by Paya and Khadga?
-Paya:
--Made from 2 words: 'Pa' which means 'to cut' (Khadga) and 'Ya' which means 'Yatra' or journey.
--It is also known as 'Khadga Chaalan' or 'Khadga Jatra' which indicates the movement with Khadga.

-Khadga:
--A Newari weapon, especially Sword.

When?
-Astami (the 8th day) in Dashain

Where?
--Valley (Kathmandu (mainly Thamel and Ason), Lalitpur, Bhaktapur)
--Lalitpur: Different Paya for Hindu and Buddhist.
--Bhaktapur: Only the Paya for Hindu.
--Kathmandu: Mainly the Paya for Buddhists.

What is done?

-Astami:
-Started on the day of Ashwin Shukla Astami.

-The goddess 'Taleju Bhawani' is taken to the main chowk.

-After that, the worship of her Khadga is done with proper rituals 'Panchopachar' at 'Dhryochhe'.

-Along with this worship, other worship such as 'Pithpuja' is done along with the worship of Lord Ganesh, Kshhetrapal, and Astabhairav.

-In Hindu Paya, 'Bhogbali' (sacrifice) is offered on this day to Devi. However, in the other Paya, the worship of gods and goddesses is done with magical rituals at Agamghar.

-The paya is taken out from Agamghar, Kotghar, or the palace at other places. However, at Thamel and Ason, it is taken out from Bikramshila Mahabihar (Bhagwan Bahal of Thamel), Bakunani of Ason, and Agamghar.

-Also, dance is performed with various musical instruments by the god's team. The God's team includes 19 people such as Swet Bhairav, Mahadev, Dumbhasingh, Indrayani, Bhadrakali, Maheshwari, Kumari, Brahmani, Ganesh, Mahakali, and Bhairav.

-At Bhaktapur, Taleju Bhawani is taken around the city and it is believed that the group of Nawadurga should assist in this.

Nawmi:
-Sacrifices are offered at Kotghar and Agamghar.

-Then, the mukut (crown) of Daitya (devil) is worn by the Thakalis.

-People also carry Kuvindo and Dhaal (shield) as it is believed that when Devi used Khadga, then the people hid in the gardens of Kuvindo (ash gourd). (But this is not found in the Paya Jatra of Ason and Thamel).

-In front of them is the team that leads the road.

-After this team, the team of Bhoot (ghosts) walk.

-The people acting as god's team are dressed in their forms.

-In this way, the team of gods with shaking bodies performs the roaming around the city with Khadga in their hands, searching for the team of devils.

Bijaya Dahsami:

-At Bhaktapur, Navdurga should go to the main chowk to get Siddhi (process: siddhiprapti) from Taleju Bhawani.

-The team of Navdruga take leave when they reach Krodh Bhairav.

-The Lasaku dhoka should be roamed around in this jatra no matter, from where the jatra started.

-In this jatra, after all the rituals are followed, then dance is necessary. Those who know how to dance should perform the actual dance and those who don't know also should move his/her feet forward as well as backward.

How was it originated?

-Story:

--In ancient times, Mahishasur was a cruel evil. No one could kill him. Thus, the gods 'Vishnu', 'Rudra', and 'Indra' created 'Devi' by combining their power. Mahishasure had a polite voice, a handsome body, and good behaviour. Hence, Devi was impressed. Hence, she couldn't defeat him in war. So, she fed him with beer and defeated him. After killing the devil and feeding him Madhu (process: Madhupan), the angry Devi took a weapon (Khadga) in her hands and went on searching whether any other person in the devil's army was to be killed.

--Believed to be started from the time of King Narendradev in Nepal. Because before 'Rato Machhindranath Jatra', the Khadga of King Narendradev was taken used.

--In the epics of Rajbanshawali, it is mentioned that when the inhabitants of Bhaktapur searched for Khadga to conduct Khadga Jatra, they got a ' sword (Khadga) having 1700 dhaal' for Siddhipuja in the palace. Thus, it can be said that this jatra was celebrated in a well-managed style in the 14th century.

Types of Paya in Kathmandu:
The various paya have 4, 8, and 12 groups of Astamatrika (eight mother goddesses who are worshipped for the elimination of obstacles resulting because of ghosts, evil spirits, and 8 great fears) on them.
Different Paya are:
-Tebaha Paya
-Batu Paya
-Mahabouddha Paya
-Kotihi Paya
-Yatakha Paya
-Banepa Paya
-Layaku Paya
-Kirtipur Paya

The differences between Paya of Thamel and Ason from other places

S.No.	Properties	Ason and Thamel	Other Parts
1	Start	Bakunani of Ason, Agamghar or Bikramshila Mahavihar.	Agamghar, Kotghar, or Palace.
2	Sacrifice	No Bhogbali on Astami	Bhogbali at Astami
3	Shield and Kuvindo	Not saw.	People carry these things during the jatra.

Differences between Madhu and Sura

S.No.	Properties	Madhu	Sura
1	Definition	The alcohol (madira) is consumed to achieve some specific aim.	The madira is consumed with personal interest.
2	Danger	Not dangerous.	Dangerous for the society and body.

3 Who	Who drinks it during the Jatra?	Drunk by gods and offered to Devi.	Drunk by devils.

References:

https://www.onlinekhabar.com/2020/10/905584

--A Newari weapon, especially Sword.

Sindure Jatra

-This jatra signifies the arrival of the spring season and the Nepali new year (Baisakh 1).

When?
-7 days from Baisakh Purnima.

Where?
Bhairavi Temple, Nuwakot

Who celebrates?
Which god is Worshipped?
Goddess Bhairavi

What is done?
-In the Mahesh Mardini temple near Bhairavi temple in Bidur municipality of Nuwakot, the worship is done for 'Lord Ganesh' and 'Dhami-Dhamini' through magical rituals by guvaju in the presence of dhami-dhamini.
-Then, the gajal is given to everyone and the jatra is started.
-Tika and Prasad are offered to everyone present there.
-After conducting 'Sindure Jatra', the goddess Bhairavi is put on the khat.
-Then, the khat is taken to Tulaja Bhawani along with dhami, dhamini, and Dware.

-Musical instruments like dhime Baja and band Baja are also blown.

-The khat of Goddess Bhairavi is also given 'Salami' on this day by the Nepal army in a 7-storeyed palace.

-This jatra ended when the goddess from Kandelchowk, Basantapur in Kathmandu is taken to Nuwakot.

-Buffalos and goats are sacrificed to the goddess 'Bhairavi'.

-Vermillion powder (Sindur) is put on the hair partition (siudo) of dhamini (Dhami's wife) during the worship.

Rath

-It is made of wood.

-It has 32 palanquins (each symbolizing different gods and goddesses) which are called khat.

Why?

-King Prithvi Narayan started this jatra in the happiness of victory over Nuwakot.

-Then, the people spread the vermillion powder over each other.

References:

https://ekantipur.com/photo_feature/2023/04/08/16809 6950504253815.html

https://www.khojnu.com/places/nepal/central-development-region/kathmandu/attractions/sindure-jatra-in-nuwakot/

https://www.explorehimalaya.com/sindure-jatra-nuwakots-best-kept-secret/

Shikali Jatra

-It is the oldest jatra celebrated during Dashain.

History of God/Goddess's Respect
-During the Licchavi and Medieval periods, many people worshipped Lord Bhairav.
-The epic 'Skanda Puran' written during the 8th century, states that from the time when Lord Shiva prayed called Mahakali, Birbhadra, and Bhairav from his jatta (tied hair), the respect for Lord Bhairav was enhanced by people.

Shikali Dance:
-Started 600 years ago.
-Conducted on the 7th day (Saptami) of Shikali Jatra.

Where?
Khokana Lalitpur

When?
Ghatasthapna (Asoj Shukla Pratipada) to Nawami

Who celebrates?
-Khokana Inhabitants

What is done?

-Dramas related to the Yagya destruction of Daksha Prajapati are presented. Some are dressed in the form of Bhairav, Mahakali, and Birbhadra and some take the form of the gods' team (Dewata gan) and show the destruction of Yagya at Shikali chaur (field). At the guthi related to Rudrayani temple, about 46 people of Devgana have surnames 'Dangol' and 'Maharjan'. They also show the play of catching the Devgana by Bhairav gana after the destruction of Yagya in the form of rounds ('Parikrama'). The next day, the Shikali dance is presented and the jatra is completed.

Procedure Followed

-The adult boys of Khokana take sugarcane and 'bhogate' in their hands and make arrangements for other equipment related to worship as well.

-On the day of Ghatasthapana in other parts, those boys eat only once and become sacred by taking bath and following rituals of worship and collection of pieces of equipment up to the morning of Tritiya (3rd day).

-From those guthis, a sacred he-buffalo is sacrificed.

-The sacred adult boys offer the blood of that he-buffalo to wake up the goddess in Shikali chaur along with some other necessary rituals.

-It's said that, previously, the dead he-buffalo used to be made alive by some magical rituals.

-Nowadays, the meat of that he-buffalo is distributed to the leader of that Guthi as well as to the other people. The different food varieties are prepared from that meat and eaten.

-On the outer part of 'ghyampo' (the jar used for making beer-jaad), a big drawing of Lord Bhairav is made.

-In that art, the 'Kasai' (one who kills the he-buffalo) puts the intestine of sacrificed he-buffalo in the form of jewels.

-After the jewel is offered, the musical instruments are blown to wake up Lord Bhairav.

-It's believed that if the blowing of musical instruments is discontinued during the rituals, Lord Bhairav doesn't come.

-Worship is done following magical rituals on the day of Ashwin Shukla Panchami.

Khasthi (6th day)

-The jatra is ended on the afternoon of Khasthi.

-When it ended, Mahakali, Bhairav, and Birbhadra start to go behind the gods' team to chase them in the whole village.

-During this time, Bhairav, Kali, and Birbhadra are at the front and the gods' team is in the front.

-There are various kinds of shaking in their body.

-The guthiyar having a Bhairav incarnation in his body carries ghyampo in his hand.

-The people take the idol of Devi Rudrayani in Khat and perform the jatra.

-The jatra is ended on reaching 'Quanlachi'.

How did it start?

-Story 1:

--Once upon a time, one tantric (with supernatural powers) king used to come to meet his lover regularly in Pachali of Teku. He used to come in the evening and return to his kingdom before the morning. As per the Newari tradition, when a person becomes older, he/she is respected as a god. Hence, she was called a goddess. One day during Dashain (Navratra), the king came as usual to meet her. That evening, she asked the king to show his 'Bhairav Avatar'. The king was worried that 'as soon as he took the "Bhairav Avatar", his lover, Aji would be fainted and wouldn't be able to bring the king to his original form. So, he asked her to ask for another wish. But Aji insisted as she had heard about the king's famous tantric energies. Thus, the king explained the rituals of bringing him from 'Bhairav Avatar' to its original form to Aji by bringing the water of the Bagmati river and taking the incarnation of Bhairav. As soon as this happened, Aji fainted. No one knew about the rituals to bring the king from 'Bhairav Awatar' to its original form except Aji. Thus, the king sat the whole night at Pachali and started his journey to his kingdom at the start of the morning. As he was tired and nobody knew how to bring him back to his original incarnation, he catches a big tree at Khokana at the bank of the Bagmati river near 'Shikali temple' and sat there. The Bhairav's incarnation in his body was not being calmed down and his body was shivering from the previous night only. In the Khokana community (basti), already many tantric used to live. On that day (Nauratha), the inhabitants were going to take bath at the bank of the Bagmati River for Nawarath. When they saw the Bhairav incarnation, they thought of converting it into the form of a jatra through their tantric energy. From that time, the Khokana community started to celebrate Shikali jatra instead of Dashain. Every 12 years, this jatra is taken to Pachali as the king is included in this jatra.

-Story 2:

In Magh Maatmayam of Skanda Puran, Daksha Prajapati insulted his daughter and son-in-law (Lord Mahadev). As Sati (his daughter) couldn't bear this, she dived into the 'Yagyakunda' (fire in Yagya/great worship) and died. When Lord Mahadev heard this through Narad, he called Kali and Bhairav along with the team of gods (dewata gan) and destroyed the Yagyakunda of Daksha Prajapati. Thus, this story is presented in the form of drama at Shikali chaur of Khokana Lalitpur for 1 week.

-Story 3:

--When Lord Buddha (who used to respect peace) saw the death of many leaving beings during Dashain, he was 'bechain' (restless). Thus, he searched for some peaceful place for peace of his mind. At that time, he reached the Rudrayani temple of Khokana and stayed there.

What makes Khokana special and Different?

-It doesn't celebrate Dashain. Instead, Shikali jatra is conducted during that time.

-First electric lamps in South Asia were lit in this village. In 1968, the electricity produced at Pharping was tested in this village by Chandra Shumsher. The first house at which the lamp was lit is still safe at Khokana.

-This village had the first experience of drinking water from 'Kaldhara' (tube wells').

-In 1958, the first school was opened in this village with 60 schools.

-This place was given more importance by the Ranas because of the facilities and cultural specialities of this area.

-Due to the availability of physical and cultural facilities at Khokana, it was called 'Jitapur' during the Lichhavi period, Medieval period (Madhyakal), and even now by some people.

-The Khokana community think of the rearing of cock, and pig as a bad sign (asuv). Hence, they don't rear these animals and birds.

-They don't celebrate Dashain as they are busy conducting the jatra at this time.

Unusual Activities in Khokana During Dashain

-No one can ring the bell in any temple during this time.

-People can't sing the song during this time.

Story for Such Unusual Activity

-Because of the animal sacrifice during Dashain, peace-loving Lord Shwayambhu was hurt. Thus, he tried to go to some peaceful place. At this time, Rudrayani temple was the best place for him. Thus, on the head of goddess Rudrayani Devi, there is the idol of Lord Shwayambhu (Karunamaya).

-It's believed that during this time when the whole of Nepal is busy giving sacrifices, this place gives the rest to the weapons.

Rudrayani Guthi

-It is the guthi of 'Dewata Khalak'.

-3 guthis take part in Shikali Jatra. They are 'Taha Guthi', 'Salagu Guthi', and 'Jaha Guthi'.

Main Day of Shikali Jatra: Ashwin Shukla Khasthi

-God Birbhadra and goddess Mahakali along with the gods' team are woken up on this day and the destruction of Yagya of Daksha Prajapati is shown.

-When the rituals of waking are completed, a member of Dewata Khalak, Birbhadra and Mahakali is woken up.

-The guthiyar (the member of guthi on whom god and goddess are woken up) who is sitting at home during this time, starts to show his behaviours.

-When people know about this, they take the guthiyar to Shikali chaur.

-In each of the 3 guthis mentioned above, there is a team of 9 people.

-The guthiyar reaches Shikali chaur by being well-dressed with cultural mukut (crown), jewels, and clothes.

-The guthiyar's hand is then washed with water and he is asked to taste the prepared beer in ghyampo.

-After that, the guthiyar starts to act as mahakali and Birbhadra.

-People believe that when the thrown rice (Bhat) in the form of Prasad (god's blessing in the form of an offering) is eaten, the diseases are eliminated.

Description of Shikali Devi

-At the bank of the Bagmati River in Khokana, there is a temple.

-In that temple, there is a large stone

-That stone is worshipped as 'Shikali Devi'.

Beliefs During Shikali Jatra:

-The thrown as Prasad helps in curing the diseases.

-Lord Bhairavi doesn't come when the blowing of musical instruments is stopped in the middle.

-In ancient times, the sacrificed he-buffalo could be made alive by performing some magical rituals.

-It generates a feeling of peace in Nepali people's hearts.
-The weapons are given rest in this place as in the other places, they are misused for making sacrifices.

References:

https://www.onlinekhabar.com/2020/10/904977
https://www.onlinekhabar.com/2022/10/1199201
https://www.onlinekhabar.com/2020/10/905029

Rato Machhindranath Jatra

-It is the longest jatra in Kathmandu Valley. Takes place for around 2 months.

-It is being celebrated for more than one thousand years.

-This is done to honour the deity 'Vajrayani Buddhism' by Buddhists too.

Where?

Valley

Who is worshipped?

-Rato Macchindranath, the god of 'Barsa and Sahakal' (Rain and).

-This god is also called Lokeshwor, Raktawalokiteshwor, Minnath Karunamaya, Karunawatar, Loknath, and Bristidev.

-He is worshipped as Harihar or Mahadev. Thus, the mridang path is done.

When?

-Baisakh Shukla Purnima

Who celebrates?

-Jyapu (Newar) Community of Nepal

What is done?

-The Lokeshwor is taken out from the party of Tahbaahal. During this time, 'Salami' is given by the paltan (group) of 'Gurujyu'.

-Mridanga Kirtan Paath (Kirtan: religious chanting or musical conversation) is done at Dawali of Tahbaahal by different groups before putting 'Bristidev' on the rath.

-While putting the Karunawatar on the rath (ratharohan), a dish (with 'om' written on it), the batti lit by one, the jhallari umbrella, and Kan baja (a musical Instrument) are taken.

-The rath is taken from Pulcok to the Sorahkhutte party.

-The rath of Minnath (20 meters) at Gahbahaal is pulled about 20 meters and taken to the Sorahkhutte party.

-While pulling the chariot and taking it around the city, wherever the rath is stopped, worship is done.

-The worship 'Chwayalabhu' is done followed by another worship 'Bhujya' on the next day.

-The rath is also taken around the 'Ama' (mother) temple of Lagankhel from Pulchok through Manglabazar. The goddess of 'Ama Mandir' is considered the mother of 'Rato Machhindranath'.

-The chariot along with the rath of Minnath is taken to Jawalakhel as well after Lagankhel.

-After showing Bhoto (a half-Tshirt in Nepal) at Jawalakhel (called as 'Bhoto Jatra ceremony'), the jatra is considered to have been completed.

-Following that, the chariot with god is taken to Bungamati during Bhadra month.

-After that, 'Machhindranath ko Nariwal Khasalne Jatra' is done on the next day after taking the rath around Lagankhel.

-4 days after the god is taken to Bungamati, the rath is broken.

Worships done During Rato Machhindranath Jatra

-At Mangalbazar 'Barahi' puja is done.

-At Gabahal, 'Durbar Puja' is conducted.

-At Lagankhel, 'Mahabali' is offered by sacrificing the he-buffalo, goat, duck, and cock.

During Corona:

'Kshhama Puja' was done for begging pardon from the god about not doing the worship following all the rituals.

References:

https://www.onlinekhabar.com/2020/07/884510
https://www.onlinekhabar.com/2020/09/894508
https://www.onlinekhabar.com/2020/09/896302
https://www.onlinekhabar.com/2022/06/1136589
https://en.wikipedia.org/wiki/Rato_Machindranath_Jatra